queer
cocktails

queer cocktails

50 cocktail recipes
celebrating gay icons
and queer culture

compiled by **lewis laney**

DOG 'n' BONE

Published in 2021 by Dog 'n' Bone Books
An imprint of Ryland Peters & Small Ltd

20–21 Jockey's Fields   341 E 116th St
London WC1R 4BW   New York, NY 10029

www.rylandpeters.com

MIX
Paper from
responsible sources
FSC   FSC® C008047
www.fsc.org

10 9 8 7 6 5 4 3 2

A CIP catalog record for this book is available from the
Library of Congress and the British Library.

ISBN: 978 1 912983 27 8

Printed in China

For recipe and photography credits,
see page 64.
Illustrator: Steve Millington aka Lord Dunsby

Commissioning editor: Kate Burkett
Senior designer: Emily Breen
Art director: Sally Powell
Head of Production: Patricia Harrington
Publishing manager: Penny Craig
Publisher: Cindy Richards

NOTES:
Recipes make enough to serve 1 unless
stated in the individual introduction.
Ice cubes or crushed ice are not stated in
ingredients but are useful for most recipes.

contents

introduction

The 50 delicious cocktails in this book pay tribute to our LGBTQ+
heroes, from times gone by right through to today—those who
have fought for gay rights, those who have provided a soundtrack
to queer life, and those who are just too darn fabulous to ignore
(Liza, here's looking at you, girl).

Whether you're raising a Dark and Stormy to the '50s heartthrob
and original angsty teenager, James Dean, toasting the world's most
famous drag queen, RuPaul, with a Silk Stocking, or having a sip of
Green Fairy while you bop along to Kylie Minogue's newest tune, you
can get your friends together, shake up the cocktails, and celebrate
these queer icons with a glass in hand!

And there are even a few recipes to help your Pride party
go off with a bang.

Happy drinking,
Lewis

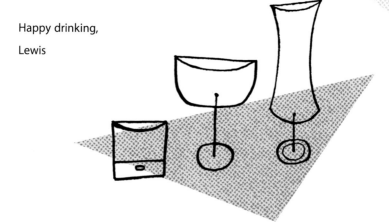

simple sugar syrup

Ingredients

Superfine (caster) sugar

Water

Before we start, here's a recipe for simple sugar syrup, which is a key ingredient in a whole host of recipes featured in the book.

Mix superfine (caster) sugar and water in equal quantities by weight and stir. The mixture will be cloudy at first but keep stirring and eventually it will form a clear syrup. This will keep in a clean, screw-top jar or bottle in the fridge for three weeks.

bloody mariah

MARIAH CAREY

Glassware

Highball

Garnish

Celery

Chili or dried hot pepper flakes

Ingredients

2 cups (500ml) tomato juice

2½ cups (400g) cherry tomatoes

2 tablespoons Worcestershire sauce

2 tablespoons hot sauce

1¼-inch (3-cm) piece of horseradish, finely grated

Sea salt and freshly ground black pepper

2oz (60ml) fresh lime juice

10oz (300ml) vodka

Along with her unmistakable voice, which hits notes other singers can only dream of, Mariah Carey is known for her self-proclaimed diva tendencies. Requests on her backstage riders have allegedly included a person employed solely to throw out her gum, an extra hotel suite to use as a wardrobe, and a bottle of champagne with bendy straws for sipping. After getting through a lot of fizz (and feeling frustrated at some of her more obscure demands not being met), Carey might well be in need of a pick-me-up, so here is the perfect hair of the dog recipe (which serves four) to get her back to her best (behavior).

Put the tomato juice and cherry tomatoes in a food processor and blend until smooth. Transfer to a pitcher and stir in the Worcestershire sauce, hot sauce, and grated horseradish. Season with salt and pepper, cover with plastic wrap, and chill in the fridge for at least 30 minutes. When ready to serve, add the lime juice and vodka, and stir well. Place a celery stick in each of the four highball glasses, fill each glass with ice, and pour in the Bloody Mariah mixture. Garnish each with a pinch of chili or dried red pepper flakes and enjoy!

black velvet

LIZA MINNELLI

Glassware

Champagne flute

Ingredients

½ glass Guinness

Champagne, to top

Life is a Cabaret for this all-singing, all-dancing actor. An over-the-top, eccentric character, Liza Minnelli's starring role in the gender-bending musical *Cabaret* cemented her position as a gay icon. Her jet-black, bowl-cut hairstyle with velvet hat perched on top is one of the most iconic looks in cinematic history and one that this cocktail, and drag queens the world over, pay homage to.

Half-fill a champagne flute with Guinness, gently top up with champagne, and serve.

old-fashioned on the rocks

ROCK HUDSON

Glassware

Rocks

Garnish

Orange zest

Ingredients

1 sugar cube

2 dashes
Angostura bitters

2oz (50ml) rye whiskey
or bourbon

Rock Hudson was the all-American movie star everyone adored, a Hollywood Giant, and one of those old-fashioned heartthrobs who the whole world wanted a cocktail date with (and, all going well, potentially some Pillow Talk).

Muddle all the ingredients in a rocks glass, adding ice as you go.

Garnish with orange zest and serve.

green fairy

KYLIE MINOGUE

Glassware

Poco grande

Ingredients

1oz (25ml) absinthe

1oz (25ml) freshly
squeezed lemon juice

1oz (25ml) chilled water

¾oz (20ml) simple
sugar syrup (see page 7)

Dash Angostura bitters

½ egg white

The LGBTQ+ community just can't get this pop icon—nor the hangover they'll inevitably suffer from after a sip of her cocktail's namesake—out of their heads. Not content with her infectious music filling dancefloors worldwide, Kylie Minogue Step(ped) Back in Time to revisit her acting career in 2001 when she starred as the Absinthe Green Fairy in Baz Luhrmann's *Moulin Rouge*. Just one of these cocktails will have you Spinning Around and away with the (green) fairies.

Fill a cocktail shaker with ice cubes and add all of the ingredients. Shake very well and strain into a chilled cocktail glass. Serve immediately.

pimm's deluxe

JULIE ANDREWS

Glassware

Collins

Ingredients

2oz (50ml) Pimm's No 1 Cup

Dash elderflower cordial

Sliced strawberries, orange, lemon, and cucumber

Well-chilled prosecco or dry sparkling wine, to top

Sprig of mint

You'd be hard pushed to think of a more quintessentially British character than Mary Poppins. Dame Julie Andrews won an Oscar for Best Actress for her title—and first—role in the film about a model English nanny. And after a long day of looking after children, how does Mary Poppins relax? Why, with a quintessentially British drink, of course!

Fill a collins glass with ice cubes and add the Pimm's, elderflower, and sliced fruit. Stir well, then half-fill with prosecco or dry sparkling wine. Stir gently, then add the rest of the prosecco or sparkling wine. Lightly crush the mint sprig and drop it in the top. Serve.

prima donna

DIANA ROSS

Glassware

Champagne flute

Ingredients

1oz (30ml) vodka

½oz (15ml) limoncello

1oz (30ml)
pomegranate juice

Well-chilled prosecco,
to top

Diana Ross has been a regular in the charts for over 50 years. With achievements such as that, her life has most certainly been turned Upside Down, earning her every right to don the prima donna crown now and again.

Put the vodka, limoncello, and pomegranate juice in a cocktail shaker and add a handful of ice cubes. Shake well and strain into a chilled champagne flute, top with prosecco, and serve.

stoli bolli

PATSY STONE

Glassware

Champagne flute

Ingredients

1oz (30ml) vodka

Well-chilled champagne,
to top

Forever 39 years old, Patsy Stone is the ultimate "fash mag slag" with a razor-sharp tongue. One half of the iconic *Absolutely Fabulous* duo, Stone is constantly shopping, brunching, and partying with her sidekick, Eddie. The pair's favorite tipple is a mixture of vodka and the finest champagne—a drink they call the "Stoli Bolli," sweetie, darling.

Fill a cocktail shaker with ice cubes and add the vodka. Shake well and strain into a chilled cocktail glass. Top with champagne and serve.

summer garden

DONNA SUMMER

Glassware

Champagne flute

Garnish

Cucumber shaving

Ingredients

1½-inch (4-cm) piece of cucumber

5 basil leaves

1 teaspoon simple sugar syrup (see page 7)

Well-chilled cava or other dry sparkling wine, to top

Donna Summer is responsible for some of the biggest disco hits of the '70s and '80s... and boy do the gays love a disco! Summer has been described as an "accidental gay icon," never actively courting a queer audience, but providing a soundtrack to the decades in which LGBTQ+ people came out of the shadows and onto the dancefloor.

Cut the cucumber into small chunks and place in a cocktail shaker with the basil and simple sugar syrup. Muddle well to release all the juice. Add ice, stir well, and then strain into a chilled champagne flute. Top with cava or sparkling wine, garnish with a long strip of cucumber, and serve.

classic champagne cocktail

AUDREY HEPBURN

Glassware

Champagne flute

Ingredients

1 brown sugar cube

Several dashes
Angostura bitters

1oz (25ml) cognac or
Grand Marnier, or a
mixture of the two

Well-chilled champagne,
to top

In *Breakfast at Tiffany's*, Audrey Hepburn plays Holly Golightly who is out to bag a millionaire in her classic LBD, pearls, and oversized sunglasses. A lady of great taste, her drink of choice can't be anything other than champagne—even before breakfast.

Coat the sugar cube with Angostura bitters and drop it into a chilled champagne flute. Chill the cognac and/or Grand Marnier in a separate glass by stirring it gently with ice cubes, then strain it into the champagne flute. Top with champagne and serve.

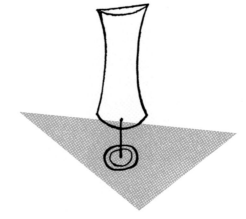

sapphire

ELIZABETH TAYLOR

Glassware

Martini

Garnish

Fresh blueberries

Ingredients

2 teaspoons parfait amour

2oz (50ml) well-chilled gin

Think of Elizabeth Taylor and the first thing that comes to mind is a deep affection for gems and marriages (plural). In 1993, Taylor even brought out a perfume named after her true loves… Diamonds and Sapphires.

Gently pour the parfait amour into a well-chilled martini glass. Pour in the gin over the rounded back of spoon, so that it forms a layer over the parfait amour. Garnish with blueberries on a cocktail stick and serve immediately.

harvey wallbanger

HARVEY MILK

Glassware

Highball

Garnish

Orange slice

Ingredients

2oz (60ml) vodka

½oz (15ml) Galliano

Orange juice, to top

Harvey Milk, was San Francisco's first openly gay elected official and during his political years he worked to make the streets, homes, bars, and places of employment a safer place for LGBTQ+ people. He also had a hand in getting the artist, Gilbert Baker, to help create the first two rainbow flags ever flown. Let's fly the flag for Milk with this wallbanger.

Build the ingredients over ice into a highball glass, stir, and serve with an orange slice.

fry martini

STEPHEN FRY

Glassware

Martini

Garnish

2 unstuffed green olives

Ingredients

½oz (15ml) dry vermouth

2½oz (75ml) vodka

Twist of lemon zest

There aren't many things Stephen Fry can't do. He's an author, actor, writer, presenter, comedian, and was once awarded Pipe-smoker of the year! Although he struggled with his sexuality in the early part of his life, now, as an openly gay man, he actively campaigns for LGBTQ+ rights.

Pour the vermouth and vodka over ice in a mixing jug. Stir to make the cocktail very cold. Strain into a martini glass. Hold the lemon zest over the glass and twist to spray a fine mist of its oils onto the cocktail. Discard the zest and garnish the martini with olives speared on a toothpick.

manhattan

MARSHA P JOHNSON

Glassware

Nick and Nora

Garnish

Maraschino cherry

Twist of orange zest

Ingredients

2oz (50ml) bourbon

1oz (25ml) sweet red vermouth

2 dashes Angostura bitters

Marsha P Johnson is remembered for being one of the original mothers of New York's gay kids, her passion for queer rights, and for the colorful flowers she wore in her hair, attracting attention as she sashayed down Christopher street. Johnson will be memorialized with a statue in New York, but until then raise a glass to this queer icon.

Fill a cocktail shaker with ice cubes, add all the ingredients except the garnish, and stir well. Strain into a chilled cocktail glass, garnish with a cherry and a twist of orange zest, and serve immediately.

english rose

PRINCESS DIANA

Glassware

Champagne flute

Garnish

Edible rose petal

Ingredients

1 teaspoon rosewater

¾oz (20ml) elderflower liqueur

½oz (15ml) gin

1 teaspoon freshly squeezed lemon juice

Well-chilled prosecco or other dry sparkling wine, to top

Legend has it that Freddie Mercury famously dressed the world's favorite princess in drag so he could smuggle her into a gay club unnoticed. This may be a side to Diana the world has never seen, but one that establishes her as a true queer icon.

Put the rosewater, elderflower liqueur, gin, and lemon juice in a cocktail shaker. Add a handful of ice and shake well. Strain into a chilled champagne flute and top with prosecco or dry sparkling wine. Garnish with a rose petal and serve.

rags to riches

DOLLY PARTON

Glassware

Rocks

Garnish

Lemon and orange zest

Ingredients

2oz (60ml) tequila, fat-washed with hazelnut brown butter (1 stick {100g} unsalted butter, handful of crushed hazelnuts, 24oz {700ml} tequila)

1 teaspoon simple sugar syrup (see page 7)

3 dashes Angostura bitters

The loveable country singer who started life in (her) Tennessee Mountain Home is the fourth of twelve children. Dolly Parton grew up so poor that her mother made her a coat out of rags, her Coat of Many Colors. Today the star now has more than 60 studio albums under her rhinestone belt, her very own theme park, Dollywood, and a West End musical, proving it takes a lot more than working the standard 9 to 5 hours to achieve lifelong success.

To make fat-washed tequila, heat the butter in a small saucepan over a medium heat until it starts to bubble and "brown." Add the crushed hazelnuts, remove the pan from the heat, and stir continuously for one minute. Add the butter and hazelnut mixture to a pitcher containing the tequila and stir. Let cool for an hour before placing in the freezer overnight. Strain out the solids the next day and store the tequila in a sealed bottle at room temperature for two weeks.

When your fat-washed tequila is ready, stir all of the drink ingredients over cubed ice in a rocks glass. Garnish with lemon and orange zest.

smoking president

MARILYN MONROE

Glassware

Rocks

Garnish

Lemon zest

Fresh lavender sprig

Ingredients

2oz (60ml) mezcal

1 teaspoon agave nectar

2 drops lavender bitters

2 drops cardamom bitters

The iconic moments from Marilyn Monroe's films are plentiful: running around with drag queens in *Some Like it Hot*, proclaiming, "Diamonds are a Girl's Best Friend" in *Gentlemen Prefer Blondes*, and enjoying the wind blowing up her white dress as she stands atop a subway grate in New York in *The Seven Year Itch*. Yet one of her most memorable performances took place on stage when she sang "Happy Birthday" to President John F Kennedy at Madison Square Gardens, New York, in a flesh-colored, rhinestone-bejeweled dress while rumors of an affair between the two swirled.

Stir all the drink ingredients over cubed ice in a rocks glass for 30–40 seconds, or until the desired level of dilution is reached. Gently squeeze the lemon zest garnish to express the citrus oils into the glass. Garnish the glass with the lemon zest and a lavender sprig.

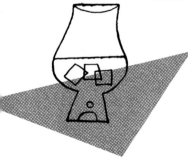

club tropicana

GEORGE MICHAEL

Glassware

Poco grande

Garnish

Pineapple slice

Ingredients

2oz (60ml) golden rum

1oz (30ml) coconut cream

½oz (15ml) light cream

1oz (30ml) pineapple juice

Don't Let the Sun Go Down on a good time. Instead, get yourself Outside, propped up by the pool, Club Tropicana in hand, just like George Michael would have wanted. In this day and age, drinks may not be free, but that doesn't mean the party has to stop. Release your inhabitations and find your Freedom with this tasty tropical cocktail.

Put all the ingredients into a blender, add a scoop of crushed ice, and blend. Pour into a glass and garnish with a thick slice of pineapple.

orange daquiri

Glassware

Martini

Ingredients

2oz (60ml) rum

⅔oz (20ml) fresh
lime juice

1 teaspoon simple
sugar syrup (see page 7)

LAVERNE COX

The *Orange is the New Black* star holds many "firsts" to her name. She is the first transgender person to appear on the cover of *Time* and *Cosmopolitan* magazines, the first transgender person to be nominated for a Primetime Emmy Award, and the first transgender person to have a waxwork at Madame Tussauds, San Francisco. I wonder if this is the first time she's had a cocktail dedicated to her?

Pour all the ingredients into an ice-filled shaker. Shake and strain into a chilled martini glass.

stiletto

Glassware

Champagne coupe

Ingredients

1oz (30ml) amaretto

½oz (15ml) freshly squeezed lime juice

Well-chilled cava or other dry sparkling wine, to top

This fierce star of *Pose*—the queer drama set in the ballrooms of '80s and '90s New York, USA—has flipped red carpet fashion on its head. Heels, capes, ball gowns, rhinestones, a hat with a beaded curtain that automatically opens and closes (presumably to block out the haters), and even wings, Billy Porter's style transcends the boundaries of both gender and fashion.

Put the amaretto and lime juice in a cocktail shaker with a handful of ice and shake well. Strain into a chilled champagne coupe, add the cava or sparkling wine, and serve immediately.

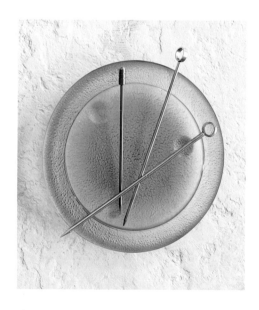

martinez

Glassware

Martini

Garnish

Lemon twist

Ingredients

2oz (60ml) gin

½oz (15ml) sweet vermouth

Dash orange bitters

Dash maraschino liqueur

Whether he was driving the entire world crazy shaking his bon-bon or playing Versace's lover in _The Assassination of Gianni Versace_, the LGBTQ+ community have always kept a close eye on this Latin hunk. For years, Ricky Martin avoided answering questions about his love life, but now he is openly Livin' La Vida Loca with his husband and their four children.

Add all the ingredients to a shaker filled with ice, shake, and strain into a chilled martini glass. Garnish with a lemon twist.

ginger rum

PRINCE HARRY

Glassware

Martini

Garnish

Lime twist

Maraschino cherry

Ingredients

1 piece stem ginger, crushed to a purée with a fork

1 teaspoon ginger syrup

2oz (60ml) golden rum

½oz (15ml) fresh lime juice

Flame haired Prince Harry and his American wife, Meghan Markle, were the first members of the Royal family to publicly celebrate Pride month, stating "love is love" in a post on their official Instagram account. Now that's definitely something to drink to!

Put the puréed stem ginger, ginger syrup, rum, and lime juice into a shaker filled with ice. Shake well, then strain into a glass filled with ice, and garnish with a maraschino cherry speared with a cocktail stick and wrapped in a twist of lime zest. Add extra syrup if you prefer a sweeter drink. Alternatively, whizz in a blender, then strain over ice.

tequila queen

FREDDIE MERCURY

Glassware

Martini

Garnish

3 coffee beans

Ingredients

2oz (60ml) añejo tequila

1oz (30ml)
coffee liqueur

1oz (30ml) espresso
(one shot)

A shy man who became one of the world's most electric frontmen as soon as he stepped on stage, Freddie Mercury definitely had A Kind of Magic about him. When you're in need of a pick-me-up after strutting your stuff on the dancefloor for hours on end, reach for this espresso-based cocktail for a sprinkle of Mercury magic. The Show Must Go On after all...

Shake all the ingredients with ice very hard in the cocktail shaker; the espresso will quickly melt the ice. Strain into a chilled martini glass and garnish with three coffee beans.

cosmopolitan

CARRIE BRADSHAW

Glassware

Martini

Garnish

Lemon zest

Ingredients

1¼oz (35ml) lemon vodka

⅔oz (20ml) triple sec

⅔oz (20ml) fresh
lime juice

1oz (25ml) cranberry juice

The original girl about town with the best bunch of brunching pals, the biggest shoe collection the small screen has ever seen, and a column in *Vogue*, Carrie Bradshaw was the Cosmo-sipping style icon we all wanted to be in the late '90s.

Add all the ingredients to a shaker filled with ice, shake, and strain into a chilled martini glass. Garnish with lemon zest for that extra zing!

death in the afternoon

ALFRED HITCHCOCK

Glassware

Champagne flute

ingredients

1½oz (35ml) absinthe

5oz (125ml) very cold champagne, to top

While Alfred Hitchcock may not be an obvious LGBTQ+ icon, his films are peppered with queerness: the questionable sexuality of Norman Bates in *Psycho*, the obvious homosexual relationship in *Rope*, and the plethora of iconic female stars he worked with (Grace Kelly, Janet Leigh, Doris Day, and Kim Novak to name but a few). Plus, the master of suspense never shied away from presenting taboo sexual themes in his movies. Drink up quick before the master of suspense finishes you off!

Pour the absinthe into a chilled champagne flute and top gently with the champagne. It will turn milky and opalescent. Serve immediately.

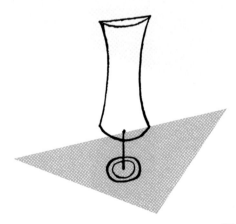

ruby slipper spritzer

JUDY GARLAND

Glassware

Highball

Garnish

Sliced strawberries

Lemon slices

Ingredients

½ oz (15ml) strawberry syrup (made with 1 cup {250ml} water, 1¼ cups {225g} white sugar, 1 cup {125g} strawberries)

1¾oz (50ml) Aperol

2½oz (75ml) fruity rosé wine, well chilled

½oz (15ml) freshly squeezed lemon juice

¾ cup (200ml) soda water

So much of Judy Garland's existence is woven into gay culture that no one can deny her icon status. "Is she a friend of Dorothy?" is an expression coined by gay men to identify each other and stems from Garland's famous character in *The Wizard of Oz*; the community have adopted the film's anthem "Somewhere Over the Rainbow" (the rainbow being the internationally recognized symbol of Pride) as their own. Click your heels together three times when in need of a drink and you'll find yourself not at home, but at the bar, Ruby Slipper Spritzer in hand.

To make the strawberry syrup, put the water in a small saucepan with the white sugar. Bring to the boil and simmer until clear and slightly thickened. Take off the heat and add the chopped flesh of the strawberries. Leave to cool, strain, discard the strawberries, and transfer the syrup to a clean screw-top jar. When your strawberry syrup is ready, pour it into a highball glass. Add the Aperol, rosé, and lemon juice, and stir. Add ice cubes and top with up with soda water to taste. Garnish with sliced strawberries and lemon slices. Serve at once.

rocket man

ELTON JOHN

Glassware

Martini

Ingredients

¼ cup (30g) fennel slices, including fronds

¼ cup (30g) packed arugula (rocket) leaves

¾oz (20ml) fresh lime juice

¾oz (20ml) simple sugar syrup (see page 7)

2oz (60ml) gin

The B***h Is Back… Has he ever really left? Loved and loathed by other queer idols (who doesn't like a bit of drama?), and after over 50 years in showbiz, Elton John is Still Standing as one of the true gay icons of our time. With 33 studio albums and seven soundtracks under his belt, this Rocket Man shows no sign of slowing down. Make your Saturday night more than alright by indulging in this delicious drink.

Add a pinch of the fennel fronds, sliced fennel, arugula leaves, lime juice, and simple sugar syrup to a cocktail shaker and muddle until the fennel is bruised. Add the gin and top with ice. Shake vigorously, then double-strain into a chilled martini glass and serve.

naked and famous

MADONNA

Glassware

Champagne coupe

Ingredients

¾oz (20ml) mezcal

¾oz (20ml) fresh
lime juice

¾oz (20ml) yellow
Chartreuse

¾oz (20ml) Aperol

Madonna is the world's best-selling female recording artist and arguably one of the most famous women on the planet. The Material Girl became queen of the gays way before it was in Vogue. Never afraid to express herself, Madonna released her famous X-rated book, *SEX*, in 1992, in which she was pictured hitchhiking naked. No doubt the Queen of Pop consumed a number of these cocktails before that shoot took place!

Combine all the ingredients in a cocktail shaker with cubed ice and shake hard. Double strain into a chilled coupe glass.

pride morning mimosa

Glassware

Champagne flute

Ingredients

½ glass champagne

2 teaspoons Grand Marnier

Fresh orange juice, to top up

No matter how and where you celebrate Pride, having a few cocktails with friends is definitely on the agenda. Start the celebrations with a Pride Morning Mimosa to get you in that party mood.

Pour the orange juice over the champagne and Grand Marnier and stir gently.

rainbow sangria

Glassware

Highball

Garnish

Fresh fruit to make a rainbow— raspberries, strawberries, oranges, pineapples, apples, blueberries, and blackberries

Ingredients

1 bottle dry red wine

⅔ cup (150ml) Grand Marnier

1 cup (250ml) orange juice

2oz (50ml) simple sugar syrup (see page 7)

3 dashes Angostura bitters

You've been marching all day, waving your banner and flying the flag at the parade, so now it's time to quench your thirst with a big pitcher of Rainbow Sangria. Make sure you've got plenty of fruit (girl, you know which kind!) and glasses for all your Pride party guests!

Add all of the ingredients to a pitcher filled with ice and stir gently to mix. Serve in glasses filled with ice, and garnish with fruit in all the colors of the Pride rainbow.

morning after the gay before

Glassware

Highball

Ingredients

2oz (60ml) scotch

2½ teaspoons fresh lemon juice

2½ teaspoons fresh lime juice

¾oz (20ml) simple sugar syrup
(see page 7)

Dash absinthe

½oz (15ml) egg white

Soda water, to top up

Pride is done and the parade is over for another year, but who says that you have to stop celebrating? Brunch the day after Pride is when you and your gang all get together to help ease the hangovers and debrief on the events of the previous day…

Combine all the ingredients, except the soda water, in a cocktail shaker with a scoop of cubed ice and shake very hard for at least 30 seconds. Strain into a glass without ice and top up with soda water, creating a foamy head on the top of the drink. Serve.

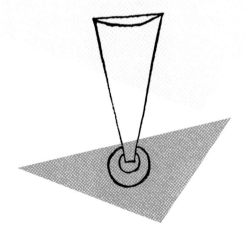

silk stocking

Glassware

Martini

Garnish

2 fresh raspberries

Ingredients

1½oz (45ml) gold tequila

½oz (15ml) white crème de cacao

½oz (15ml) heavy cream

1 teaspoon grenadine

RuPaul Andre Charles is famous for being the drag mother to hundreds of drag children who have walked her runway on *RuPaul's Drag Race*, where queens compete on the catwalk to become America's next drag superstar. One sip of this Silk Stocking and you'll soon be working it like a Cover Girl. Yaaaas Queen!

Put all the ingredients apart from the raspberries in a blender, add two handfuls of ice cubes, and blend for 20 seconds. Pour the mixture into a chilled glass, garnish with the raspberries, and serve.

i will always love woo woo

WHITNEY HOUSTON

This cocktail celebrates superstar Whitney Houston and will definitely make you Wanna Dance with Somebody!

Glassware

Highball

Garnish

Lime wedge

Ingredients

2oz (50ml) vodka

1oz (25ml) peach schnapps

4oz (100ml) cranberry juice

Few drops of fresh lime juice

Fill a cocktail shaker with ice and add the vodka, schnapps, cranberry, and lime juice. Shake well, then strain into a glass with extra ice, garnish with a lime wedge, and serve.

purple haze

Glassware

Shot

Ingredients

½ lime

1 white sugar cube

2oz (60ml) vodka

Dash of Grand Marnier

1oz (30ml) Chambord

A colorful character, Prince presented his music and persona with dazzling visual flair. His androgyny confused many, but in the LGBTQ+ community his difference and willingness to transgress boundaries was what appealed to—and resonated with—them. Prince's fondness for suggestive wordplay is evident in his song titles, so let's hope he'd approve of this cocktail, which is a play on one of his greatest hits, "Purple Rain."

Cut the fresh lime half into quarters, place them and the sugar cube in a shaker and crush them together with a muddler. Add the vodka and Grand Marnier. Fill the shaker with ice, then shake and strain the mixture into a chilled shot glass. Float a single measure of Chambord on to the drink and serve.

viva españa

PEDRO ALMODÓVAR

Glassware

Small wine glass

Garnish

Orange slice

The powerful, colorful characters in Pedro Almodóvar's movies are forces to be reckoned with—much like this cocktail. Once you've mixed this drink up and sunk some down, you might find yourself needing a siesta.

Pour the red wine, Dubonnet, orange juice, and sugar syrup into an ice-filled cocktail shaker and shake well. Strain into a small wine glass and top with cava or sparkling wine. Garnish with an orange slice and serve.

Ingredients

1oz (30ml) Spanish red wine

½oz (15ml) Dubonnet

1oz (30ml) freshly squeezed orange juice

Dash simple sugar syrup (see page 7)

Well-chilled cava or other dry sparkling wine, to top

swedish glögg

ABBA

Glassware

Small glass tankards

Garnish

Small raisins and slivered (sliced) almonds

Peel of small unwaxed orange

Ingredients

1 bottle red wine

½ bottle ruby port

1 cup (250ml) brandy

2 tablespoons light brown sugar

1 tablespoon whole cardamom pods, crushed

6 cloves

1 cinnamon stick

Take a Chance on this delicious drink celebrating the Swedish foursome, who took the world by storm in 1974 when they won the Eurovision Song Contest with "Waterloo." Serving 20, this cocktail is the perfect party punch and is sure to transform anyone who drinks it into a Dancing Queen. Now, Gimme! Gimme! Gimme! the glögg!

Using metal tongs hold the orange peel over a flame on the cooktop (hob) until it spots brown. Drop it into a large pan. Add the wine, port, brandy, sugar, and spices. Simmer over a medium heat for about 20 minutes then strain into a heatproof pitcher. Pour into small heatproof glasses and add a few raisins, almond slivers, and a twist of orange peel to each serving to garnish.

white lady

KATE BUSH

Glassware

Martini

Ingredients

1oz (30ml) freshly
squeezed lemon juice

1oz (30ml) Cointreau

1½oz (45ml) gin

½ egg white (optional)

When you think of *Wuthering Heights* you
either conjure up a picture of a ghostly woman
roaming the moors in search of Heathcliff, or
an energetic, wide-eyed woman in a white
dress, singing and dancing in the mist…
the latter being the unmistakable singer-
songwriter, Kate Bush. This zesty, gin based
cocktail would have been a welcome tipple for
both Catherine Earnshaw—after wandering
the moors at night—and Kate, once filming for
her music video finished.

Fill a cocktail shaker with ice cubes and add all
the ingredients. Shake very well, then strain into a
chilled cocktail glass. Serve immediately.

dark and stormy

JAMES DEAN

Glassware

Tumbler

Garnish

Lime wedges

Ingredients

2¼oz (60ml) rum

Ginger beer, to top up

Limes

When James Dean played a brooding, disillusioned teenager in *Rebel Without a Cause*, it was probably the first time Hollywood had dealt with adolescence in such a head-on fashion. Dean's classic look of jeans, white t-shirt, and pompadour haircut was the uniform of teenagers throughout the 1950s and early '60s, and his dark and stormy temperament is still adopted by many today.

Fill a chilled glass with crushed ice. Pour in the rum and top with ginger beer. Finish with a squeeze of lime, garnish with a lime wedge, and serve.

brooklyn   BARBRA STREISAND

Glassware

Champagne coupe

Garnish

Maraschino cherry

Ingredients

1½oz (45ml) whiskey

½oz (15ml) dry vermouth

1 teaspoon Amer Picon

1 teaspoon cherry liqueur

Lemon zest

Born and bred in Brooklyn, Barbra Streisand got her first break into show business when she won a talent contest in a Manhattan gay club and was subsequently signed up to sing there for the next few weeks. From that day on, Streisand sang and acted her way to super stardom, winning two Oscars, eleven Golden Globes, and countless Grammy Awards. Always supportive of her LGBTQ+ fans, this cocktail pays tribute to the iconic Funny Girl's roots.

Combine all the drink ingredients in a mixing glass with a scoop of cubed ice. Stir for about 30 seconds before straining into a chilled coupe glass. Squeeze the lemon zest to express the citrus oils over the drink and discard. Garnish with a cherry.

the americano

BRITNEY SPEARS

Glassware

Highball

Garnish

Orange or lemon slice

Ingredients

1oz (25ml) Campari

1oz (25ml) sweet vermouth

Soda water, to top up

To many of her fans, Britney Spears is the embodiment of the "American Dream"—a girl from Louisiana who became one of the biggest performers on the planet. This cocktail celebrating the southern star is anything but Toxic, however, and will have you saying, "Hit Me (with another one) Baby One More Time!"

Fill a glass with ice cubes, pour in the Campari, vermouth, and soda water, then stir. Add an orange or lemon slice and stir, then serve immediately.

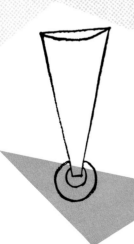

dusty nail

DUSTY SPRINGFIELD

Glassware

Rocks

Ingredients

3oz (90ml) Scotch whiskey

3oz (90ml) Drambuie

Always admired by the LGBTQ+ community, there was a brief resurgence in Dusty's popularity when she collaborated with the Pet Shop Boys in the late '80s that cemented her role as a much-loved queer icon. This recipe certainly gave Dusty The Look of Love and serves four, so when you Just Don't Know What to Do with Yourself get some friends round for a night of cocktails and karaoke.

Divide the whiskey and Drambuie between four ice-filled glasses and stir.

elderflower collins

JOAN COLLINS

Glassware

Highball

Garnish

Lemon slice

Mint sprig

Ingredients

2oz (60ml) gin

1oz (30ml) fresh lemon juice

½oz (15ml) elderflower cordial

Soda water, to top up

Simple sugar syrup (see page 7), to taste

Known for big shoulder pads, big hair, and her role in the biggest melodrama in the world, how could this English actor not feature as a queer icon? Starting out on stage as a child, Dame Joan Collins became a household name in the 1980s playing Alexis Carrington—a scheming, conniving, narcissistic, and ruthless character—on *Dynasty*. This gin-based cocktail matches Collins for sharpness and bite, which she encapsulated in this infamous villain.

Build all the ingredients into a highball glass filled with ice. Stir gently and garnish with a lemon slice and a sprig of mint.

whiskey mac

SIR IAN MCKELLEN

Glassware

Tumbler

Garnish

A twist of lemon zest

Ingredients

2oz (50ml) whiskey

2oz (50ml) green
ginger wine

Sir Ian McKellen's great great grandfather, Robert Lowes, helped invent the modern weekend, giving workers an extra half day off a week—more time to let their hair down and pour themselves a drink!

Shake the whiskey, ginger wine, and ice cubes in a cocktail shaker. Strain into a small glass and serve with a twist of lemon zest.

bey's knees

Glassware

Champagne coupe

Ingredients

1oz (25ml) freshly
squeezed lemon juice

¾oz (20ml) honey syrup
(½ cup {140g} runny
acacia honey, ⅙ cup
{40ml} hot water)

2oz (50ml) dry gin

Beyoncé always puts Love on Top. She and her husband, Jay-Z, have worked—and continue to work—tirelessly to promote equal rights for LGBT people, which won them the GLAAD Vanguard Award in 2019. When toasting to her queer fans, Queen B will reach for this cocktail, which truly is the bee's knees.

First make the honey syrup. Combine the honey and hot water in a heatproof bowl and stir until completely mixed. Half-fill a cocktail shaker with ice and add the lemon juice, honey syrup, and gin. Shake vigorously until chilled and strain into a glass. Serve immediately.

hurricane

GRACE JONES

Glassware

Hurricane

Garnish

Passion fruit seeds

Ingredients

2oz (50ml) dark rum

1oz (25ml) fresh
lemon juice

1oz (25ml) passion
fruit syrup

Passion fruit juice
(optional)

From one of her very first performances in 1977 in a members-only gay disco, Grace Jones had the crowd onside when she sang "I Need a Man" to them, for them, and as them, afterward exclaiming, "I don't know about you, honey, but I need a f*****g man!" Just years before it had been illegal for two men to so much as dance together in New York, yet here was Jones celebrating the queer community and facilitating a wind of change.

Add all the ingredients to a cocktail shaker filled with ice and shake vigorously to mix. Strain into a hurricane glass filled with crushed ice, top up with passion fruit juice, if using, and serve garnished with passion fruit seeds.

spicy margarita

SPICE GIRLS

Glassware

Champagne coupe

Garnish

1 chile de árbol

Ingredients

1⅔oz (50ml) mezcal

2oz (60ml) fresh
pomegranate juice

1¼oz (35ml) fresh
lemon juice

1¼oz (35ml) egg white

¾oz (20ml) vanilla syrup

Pinch sea salt

4 dashes hot sauce

**Spice Up Your Life with this spicy cocktail
inspired by Ginger, Sporty, Baby, Scary, and
Posh. If you Wannabe part of their gang, you
need to be a feisty feminist who can sink a drink
or two. Girl Power!**

Add all the ingredients to a cocktail shaker.
"Dry" shake without ice first then add ice and shake
a second time. Double strain into a chilled coupe
glass. Garnish with a chile de árbol.

whiskey highball

DAVID BECKHAM

Glassware

Highball

Garnish

Lemon zest

Ingredients

2oz (60ml) whiskey

Soda water, to top up

Forget bending it like Beckham, how about breaking it like Beckham? David Beckham has always been adept at curling a soccer ball, but when it came to the barrier of homosexuality in the sport, he broke straight through it, embracing his gay icon status—go on, Golden Balls! A co-creator of Haig Club Whisky, it seems fitting to dedicate this cocktail to the super-skilled soccer star.

Fill a highball glass with large ice cubes and carefully pour the whiskey down the side of the glass so that it does not touch the top of the ice. Add the soda slowly in the same manner and stop filling once the soda reaches around ⅓ inch (1cm) from the top of the glass. Use a bar spoon to mix the whiskey and soda by placing the spoon between the ice and glass and moving the spoon up and down or in a circular motion for about 5–10 seconds. Garnish with lemon zest to add aroma to the drink.

the impressionist LADY GAGA

Glassware

Champagne flute

Ingredients

½oz (15ml) Grand Marnier cherry

½oz (15ml) raspberry syrup

1 teaspoon violet liqueur

Well-chilled dry champagne, to top up

From playing the part of Mother Monster emerging from an alien egg at the Grammy's, to a love struck singer-songwriter in *A Star is Born*, a jailbird murderer in the music video for "Telephone," and a rich vampire in Ryan Murphy's *American Horror Story Hotel*, Lady Gaga (real name Stefani Germanotta) was Born (This Way) to take on many different personas. A queer ally from the outset of her career, Gaga has always flown the rainbow flag for her fans.

Fill a cocktail shaker with ice cubes. Add the Grand Marnier cherry, raspberry syrup, and violet liqueur and shake well. Strain into a chilled cocktail glass and top up with champagne. Serve immediately.

silver bronx

JENNIFER LOPEZ

Glassware

Champagne coupei

Ingredients

2oz (50ml) gin

Dash dry vermouth

Dash sweet vermouth

2oz (50ml) fresh
orange juice

1 egg white

A singer, dancer, actor... and learning to pole dance at 50 years old, Jennifer Lopez can do it all. Never one to deny her roots, Jenny From the Block is proud of growing up in the Bronx, and her rags to riches rise to fame.

Shake all the ingredients vigorously over ice and strain into a chilled cocktail glass.

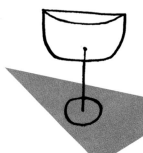

sour italian

DONATELLA VERSACE

Glassware

Champagne flute

Ingredients

1oz (30ml) Campari

½oz (15ml) Strega

½oz (15ml) Galliano

1oz (30ml) fresh
lemon juice

½oz (15ml)
cranberry juice

½oz (15ml) simple sugar
syrup (see page 7)

Dash egg white

2 dashes Angostura
bitters

At age 11, Donatella was told two important things by her brother, Gianni: that he was gay, and that she needed to become a blonde. Since then, her name has become synonymous with both supporting the queer community and waist-length, bleach-blonde hair.

Shake all the ingredients over ice and strain into a chilled champagne flute.

brandy alexander

ALEXANDER THE GREAT

Glassware

Martini

Garnish

Nutmeg

Ingredients

2oz (60ml) brandy

½oz (15ml) crème de cacao (dark or white)

½oz (15ml) heavy (double) cream

There will forever be a question mark over the sexuality of this successful military commander, but regardless of whether Alexander kept his men busy in the bedroom or on the battlefield, there's a reason his name was "Great."

Shake all the ingredients over ice and strain into a frosted martini glass. Garnish with a sprinkle of nutmeg and serve.

index

RECIPE CREDITS

PICTURE CREDITS